Follow *What* Leader?

Follow *What* Leader?

✦

A Logical Look at the Lessons of Leadership

Jim Weaver

iUniverse, Inc.
New York Lincoln Shanghai

Follow *What* Leader?
A Logical Look at the Lessons of Leadership

iUniverse books may be ordered through booksellers or by contacting:

iUniverse
2021 Pine Lake Road, Suite 100
Lincoln, NE 68512
www.iuniverse.com
1-800-Authors (1-800-288-4677)

ISBN-13: 978-0-595-39037-3 (pbk)
ISBN-13: 978-0-595-83427-3 (ebk)
ISBN-10: 0-595-39037-4 (pbk)
ISBN-10: 0-595-83427-2 (ebk)

Printed in the United States of America

Contents

PREFACE

◆

Why Another Book On Leadership?

Probably the only compilations in the book store that collect more dust than books on leadership are cookbooks. So why write another? The answer is simple. Although cooked chicken is still chicken, everyone has their own ideas about how to make it taste more interesting, more unique, and more tasty than the other guy. So it is with the subject of leadership. Perhaps there *is* nothing new under the sun. Maybe all that can be said has already been recorded. But leadership, like chicken, can be floured, spiced, and served in a myriad of ways. So, given that as my motivation, I would offer up my own logical look at the lessons of leadership. Read it, save it in its entirety, or simply paste bits and pieces of it into your own leadership recipe book. Leadership development is not rocket science, but it does take work. My intent here is simply to provide a directed learning path which is paved with ideas that will make the learning curve appear less ominous.

ACKNOWLEDGEMENTS

No project of this type is ever accomplished as a single effort. Without the help of the following people, I would have experienced much more difficulty in writing "**Follow *What* Leader?**" Barbara O'Riley-Harless assisted me in both the graphics and computer technology areas. Terry Johnston contributed with her proofreading skills, and Sandy Smith captained the final proofreading and editing effort.

A multitude of working managers and leaders provided me with ideas and examples, and demonstrated for me that "leadership" is still alive and well in many of today's organizations. Although too numerous to mention, you know who you are. My heartfelt thanks go out to you.

Jim Weaver

1

It's Not The Size Of The Dog In The Fight. It's The Size Of The Fight In The Dog.

✦

(Developing a Leadership Attitude)

My dog is dumb—at least in one respect. She's a West Highland White terrier who stands less than 12 inches high, weighs a total of 21 pounds, and couldn't hold her own in a fight with the family cat. But don't tell *her* that. She fancies herself the Muhammad Ali of the K-9 world, and sees the Doberman down the street as nothing more than a "girlie-man" mutt. I have seen her break loose and run half a block just to face down another neighborhood dog, that could easily squash her like a bug.

But she doesn't care. Because she's convinced that it's not the size of the dog in the fight. It's the size of the fight in the dog.

Leadership begins with an attitude. Call it self-assurance, confidence, sureness, poise, courage, or even arrogance, but leaders have it. They are generally winners, to be sure, but simply winning is not their goal. They just want to get into the fight. They want to mix it up, stir the pot, put a new spin on the old, and shuck and jive their way into the "lead dog" position.

Leadership is not for everybody. Even those of us who teach the skills may not be equipped to assume long-term leadership positions. During my later years as a law enforcement officer, I was afforded the opportunity to sit in the leadership "cat bird" seat. As a staff assistant, I watched our organizational leaders from a special vantage point as they worked their way through daily struggles with personnel issues, operational entanglements, and political hurdles. It very much affected my previous views of leadership, and how it is applied in the workplace.

Further, it convinced me that I was perhaps better suited for the classroom than the corporation.

When we teach leadership skills in class, we are afforded the opportunity to break them down, analyze them, and apply them to antiseptic situations which have been specifically developed for the teaching environment. It is very much like when I was on the wrestling team in college. We practiced single moves first, then doubles and combinations, then transitions from one position to another, all in unison, and all by the numbers. It always worked great during drills. The problem came when you stepped into the ring to face an opponent who was just as well trained, and who knew all of the same moves you knew. Sometimes the most pristine and practiced wrestling techniques got messy and ugly during a match.

It is the same in the day-to-day world of leadership. Learning and mastering certain leadership skills is a management must. But I'm almost willing to concede that those skills take a second place to that "attitude" which is so critically important to anyone who aspires to leadership.

You simply gotta want it! My terrier invests absolutely no  time deciding what her odds are. She wastes no energy deciding how big the other dog is, or what her chances for victory might be. She sees that the gate is open, and the chance for confrontation exists. She smells trouble and makes a bee line for it. As I said earlier, she may be dumb, but you have to admire the attitude. And there must be something to it, because there are a significant number of terriers around, and they all strut their stuff in the same way.

It all comes down to a mind-set. Do you have it? Are you willing to jump into the organizational fray regardless of the odds? There are a few indicators which I have discovered that most leaders possess in some form or other. If you think you are inclined toward leadership, perhaps you should engage in some gut-check answers relative to the questions below:

1. Is the idea of being assigned a formal leadership position in my organization totally exciting to me?

2. Even if I don't get the assignment, do I look for ways to be an informal leader among my peers?

3. Have I read and studied the different theories on leadership so that I can apply them when the opportunity presents? (Oh, you didn't know there were some theories on leadership? Well, you better get busy.)

4. Do I possess a balance between my "task-centered" focus and my "people-centered" focus?

5. Am I willing to risk being branded a failure just for a chance to try my hand at the leadership game?

6. Do I understand that leadership brings with it a form of power which must be ethically applied, and for which I am willing to be accountable?

7. Am I willing to concede that leadership and popularity are not always synonymous? And how much do I care about that?

8. Do I have the confidence to roll with the political punches, and do I realize I can't win every battle?

9. Am I flexible enough in my own leadership confidence to realize that others also have good ideas from which I can learn?

10. Do I wake up each day with a fire in my belly (not a belly ache), and actually look forward to the new challenges that await me?

Unfortunately, there are too many people in leadership positions who resemble the Old English bulldog I once owned. Effie Mae was content to spend every minute of every day eating, drinking, sleeping and passing gas. She would never have suffered at length from an ulcer because if one developed, she would simply have laid down in the corner until it went away. She was a great dog, but she was certainly no terrier. People with "English bulldog" attitudes make lousy leaders. They may have the skills. They may even possess the desire. But they fall far short when it comes to disposition, temperament, and the absolute excitement which is necessary to meet the daily challenges of leadership.

My wife will soon be at a point in her professional career where she will be faced with the decision of whether or not to take the helm of a public safety organization. It will be interesting to watch her wade through that wrenching decision-making process. Having faced such a decision in the past, I have offered her only one piece of advice...and that is this. Choose ahead of time whether or not you wish to serve in a leadership role. Know well ahead of being asked whether you are willing, able, and excited about assuming such a responsibility.

Be sure that you have answered the above-listed questions to your own satisfaction, and that the thought of leading an organization makes you tremble with anticipation. If you do not have that "terrier" attitude, you will accept your new position with hesitancy, uncertainty, and fear. You may or may not be successful, but, without a doubt, you will certainly be miserable. And that is no way to spend a career.

**Be the lead dog...**

- Either get into the leadership game, or stay out. If you wait until all uncertainty is eliminated, you have waited too long.

- Know ahead of time whether you really want a leadership position. Mamby—pamby leadership is about as appetizing to subordinates as a lukewarm cola.

- Remember that leadership isn't as clean in the workplace as it is in the classroom. Be ready to get your hands dirty in order to get the job done.

2

I Love You. Do You Love Me?

✦

(The Desire to be a Popular Leader)

Linda Dittsworth was the prettiest girl in the fourth grade. One day during Civics class, I sent her a note that read, "I love you. Do you love me?" I signed it "Love, Jimmy." It would be a romantic little puppy-love story if she had been the single recipient of my note. Unfortunately, I am embarrassed to admit that I sent similar notes to Mary Jane, Lynn, Debbie, Linda O., Linda C., Andrea, Sally, and even Anna (who was the ugliest girl in the class).

Was it a serious search for affection? Not really. Years later I came to realize what "love" really was. But was it a frivolous act? Absolutely not. It was a young boy looking for some sort of affirmation that he was valued, accepted, popular, and a respected part of his peer group. Anyone who has spent any time delving into the subjects of self-esteem and self-help realizes that we, as adults, are really not much different from that fourth grade boy. We spend immeasurable amounts of time and energy ensuring that we are loved, and secure in the knowledge that we are positively accepted and respected by others.

When I was in high school, we had this ritualistic practice of placing pictures in the yearbook of the five or six couples who were predicted "most likely to succeed." Although it may not be universally true, our pictured couples were almost always the top football players, the prettiest cheerleaders, and the smartest boy and girl in the school. I suspect little time was spent speculating about their actual propensity for success. They were just the most popular kids at the time.

I never got nominated. As much as it may sound like sour grapes, it is not. My point is simply that being accepted, and being popular, was important then, and it is important now. We constantly measure ourselves against others to determine our success, and we relish the attention we receive. Popularity is not a child's pipe dream. It is real. It is important. But it sometimes interferes with leadership.

Leadership is not a popularity contest. It isn't a contest at all. It is a somewhat complicated process which is measured by how well a leader is able to accomplish meaningful things through other people.

One of the most interesting leaders I have ever known is a middle-manager in a moderately large organization. I found her an interesting study because she has, at times, been the most hated manager to walk the floors of the office building. I was amused recently when she was appointed to assume management of a reputedly lazy, ineffective operational unit. When asked by one of her new employees if things would be changing much, she replied by saying, "Young man, all life as you presently know it is about to cease to exist." Now, how long do you think it took that unpopular statement to travel the grapevine? Certainly it was a wake-up call for that specific employee as well as the others in the unit. And it did little to elevate her popularity as a leader. But for those of us who knew her, it was little more than a surface ripple. Our experience with her leadership style told us that once she had resuscitated the unit, and instilled in them a new sense of direction and desire to work, she would not only be well-liked, but successful as a manager and leader.

For the person who seeks success as a leader, there are a number of pertinent questions s/he must answer to determine the importance to him/her of "popularity" leadership vs. "nose to the grindstone" leadership:

1. How important is it for me to be a part of the group?

2. Am I willing to stand up for what I believe regardless of the criticism I might receive?

3. Can I handle it when my subordinates show obvious disdain for me, both personally and professionally?

4. Can I always make decisions that are best for my organization regardless of the impact on my employees?

5. Will I be happy with a 65% approval rating from others? (The President of the United States is usually elated with such a rating.)

6. Can I say "no" over and over, regardless of how unfashionable it may be?

7. Can I "face down" the naysayers and ne'er-do-wells who drag down my good and loyal subordinates?

8. Can I look beyond the dark clouds of dissention, and see the light of my leadership on the horizon?

9. Can I put it away at the end of the day, or does the "lonely at the top" syndrome cause me continual anxiety?

The answers to these questions may be obvious, but the practice of leadership according to their dictates can be tedious and burdensome at times.

Some years back, a great comedy hit the silver screen. In it, a retired military Major was tasked with the monumental challenge of turning what he referred to as a "gaggle of maggots" into a well-precisioned R.O.T.C. military drill team. It goes without saying that his subordinates' final destination was a far cry, and a painful journey, from where they started. As a result, the major's life was also ruffled as he attempted to change the attitudes, priorities, and practices of his subordinates. He was neither liked nor appreciated…at least in the beginning. His success derived directly from his willingness to be unpopular as long as it took to get the job done. It was an entertaining movie, but the message for leaders is abundantly clear. If popularity and acceptance are so important to you that you are unwilling to make the hard decisions which inevitably will be required, then you might want to look elsewhere for a way to measure success. As Wall Street mogul Gordon Gecko said in the movie *Wall Street*, "It's not always the most popular guy who gets the job done."

Oh, by the way, just to end the story, I got affirmative answers from all the girls in fourth grade except for two—the prettiest and the ugliest. The prettiest said she liked me, but she was really in love with Darryl B., the blond-haired, blue-eyed transfer student whom all of us boys hated. The ugliest girl, Anna, said she could never love a boy who made faces at her and joined with the other guys in calling her "Anna Panna, fat in the canna, stinky banana beach cabana."

So there you are. You win some, you lose some, but you keep on pitching. That's what leadership is all about. That's the reason you have to love it, and it's the reason you have to feel pretty good about yourself. Because there will be times in your leadership journey when you may be the *only* one who does.

Be the lead dog...

- Leadership is not for the weak. There will be times when you are your only support group. Be ready to deal with it.

- Leadership means making the best decision for the organization you serve. If it works out well for the subordinate too, great. If not, integrity requires that you put the organization first.

- It is always easier to be a tough leader first and soften later than to do it the other way around.

3

School's Out, School's Out. Teacher Let The Fools Out.

◆

(The Importance of Leadership Training)

Remember my terrier I spoke of in chapter one? Well, she is the only dog I've ever owned that got a DNF (did not finish) in obedience school. The trainer said, "She's just not interested in learning. She thinks she knows it all already." I couldn't help but think, "Gee, that's just like some leadership people I know." Contrary to the edicts of the Genetic Theory of Leadership, leaders are not born. They are the ultimate result of a process. That is to say, they *learn* how to be leaders, and they do it by following three proven techniques: **1. Basic Training, 2. Application Of That Training, and 3. Continual Re-training.**

Basic Training

I will submit that, due to political pressures, financial incentives, compromises, and/or just because Uncle Seth plays golf with the owner of the company, some people land in leadership positions who have no more leadership talent than the good Lord gave a lima bean. Those are the harsh realities of the working world which will never go away. But overnight wonders are as obvious as a wart, and remind me of a bottle rocket on the fourth of July. Yeah, it's bright and intense when you first fire it off, but it only lasts for a short period of time. Then all that remains is a burned out cardboard tube which is ready for the scrap heap. Good leadership skills are not obtained in this manner.

Truth be known, the teacher never *did* let fools out. The only fools were the ones who didn't seek the education in the first place, or who dropped out somewhere along the way. Education and training is critically important, and not just in the field of leadership. It doesn't matter whether you choose to be a plumber or a philosopher. Neither your pipes nor your philosophies will hold water without the appropriate training. Most of us would never think to put our children behind the wheel of a car without some type of driver safety training. None of us in our right mind would ride on a 747 with a pilot who was not properly trained, and most of us seek guidance when encountering a task with which we are unfamiliar. So what on earth makes people believe they are ready to lead just because they were dropped into a leadership slot?

Talk to any leader worth his/her salt and s/he will tell you in a minute that training is the genesis of success. There was a time when it wasn't. When I first entered the work force, little leadership training even existed in the public safety milieu. But such is not the case anymore. If you would aspire to be an effective leader, here are some questions you might ask yourself relative to your own education and training readiness:

1. What do I know about leadership at this very moment in time?

2. What have I done in my life to this point that would help me qualify as a leadership candidate? (List them.)

3. How many books on leadership do I own, and how many have I read?

4. How many classes, seminars, and schools have I attended that taught me something about leadership?

5. Where are the notes that I took in those classes, and when was the last time I reviewed them?

6. How many people do I know that I could access quickly to assist me in my leadership education?

7. Does any part of my post-secondary education include elements of management or leadership training?

8. Am I willing to invest my own time and money to secure the proper leadership education and training?

9. What are my weaknesses in the field of leadership, and what can I do to shore them up?

10. Do I have the energy to study to become a good leader, or am I simply content to hold the title?

Too many people assume that leadership knowledge comes naturally. First you crawl, then you walk, and eventually you run marathons. Actually, there probably have been a few who have learned leadership by that slow, antiquated process. But it is no longer necessary. Today's world is a fast-paced, unforgiving, high-expectancy arena. Those who choose to compete and win must be willing to make the initial investment in education and training. It is not optional. It is a necessity. No one wants a cop to respond to their emergency who can't fight, can't shoot, and can't make life and death decisions. No one wants a firefighter to come to their fire who can't hook up a fire hose, climb a ladder, or work an oxygen tank. And no one has any use for a leader who wants the part, looks the part, but in the final analysis doesn't have the basic skills to do what needs to be done.

Application of that training

Some years back, I went to real estate school. It had nothing to do with my profession, and I had no real plans to use the license once I secured it. In fact, the only reason I even signed up was because my girlfriend wanted to go and I wanted to be with her. But I went, and I passed, and I took a state board which then permitted me to practice real estate anywhere I chose inside the state. And that's where it ended. I put the books on a shelf, filed the license away in my drawer, and with the exception of a re-certification course that I take every two years, I have had nothing to do with real estate since. Except for the fact that I did keep the girlfriend .

So what's the point? Simply this. I got the basic training as required above. It was good training which prepared me to successfully meet the requirements to become a realtor. But because I never followed through with the application of my new-found knowledge, I don't know diddly squat about real estate today and would be a very poor realtor, even though I have a license that says I am one.

Application of leadership knowledge can be looked at from two different, yet equally important, perspectives. First is the willingness to try the new leadership ideas to which you have been exposed. It is an unfortunate reality that people go to school, learn new theories and approaches, become convinced of their effectiveness, yet go back into the workplace and continue business in the same inefficient and ineffective manner as before.

When it comes to the game of golf, I would have to improve some before I would qualify for the moniker "duffer." Like many enthusiasts, I understand the game, and like the game, but fail miserably when attempting to direct the path of my ball. My brother, who by the way, is a golf professional, has attempted more than once to correct my style. He tells me that my grip on the club is "lazy" and could be corrected by rolling my right hand over the top of the club. It sounds easy enough, but it feels funny. In other words, to make my grip stronger I need to *apply* some new knowledge which is outside my comfort zone.

Do I know what I am doing wrong? Yes. Have I learned what I need to do to correct it? Yes. Am I willing to do it? No. Hence, I am a lousy golfer with a comfortable grip. Change is uncomfortable. It requires flexibility, persistence, and a certain amount of discomfort each time it is implemented. The application of a new leadership technique is no different, in some respects, than correcting a golf swing. The sad part is that the application process pressures too many potentially good leaders to quietly admit that, although they thought they wanted a leadership career, it turns out they just wanted a paycheck.

The willingness to integrate new knowledge into your leadership style is a critical step in the learning process. It is, as I stated earlier, the integration of your rehearsed wrestling moves into a real wrestling match. It gives you a chance to see what works, what doesn't, and what needs to be tweaked in order to be successful.

The second characteristic of the application process is what I call "organizational maturity." That simply means hanging around in your organization long enough to gain some level of institutional knowledge. I would never have believed this when I was a young manager because I wanted to climb the organizational ladder as high as I could, as fast as I could. It was only when I got stalled in one management position for several years that it became abundantly clear that you can learn a great deal just by coming to work every day, doing your job, and watching how the organization rises, falls, tumbles and spins under different types of leadership. Although it doesn't seem so, spending time in grade is actually a shortcut to success. It gives you the opportunity to watch what works well, and what fails, without actually having to experiment with everything yourself.

As a young middle manager I was constantly frustrated by the men and women at the top who seemed to consistently make daily decisions which interfered with our operational capacity to do the job. It seemed that every policy was a watered-down version of what we needed, and executive management never veered far from the middle of the road even when drastic measures were necessary. It was only after years of experience that I learned of the need for executive leaders to make decisions, not just for operational capacity, but also for political expediency. It is an education that does not come in the classroom, but one that is integral to your success as a manager and leader. Good things like cheese, wine, and leadership talent simply take time to create.

Continual Re-training

My daughter has a fish tank in her bedroom which holds just enough of those little black guppy things to procreate and to keep the tank filthy. The ongoing battle is that my wife insists on cleaning the fish tank filter in the kitchen sink instead of outside with the garden hose. When I walked into the kitchen the other day, I spotted the geometric plastic parts from the fish tank filter lying on the drainboard. I snatched them up, took them to my daughter's bedroom, and threw them onto the floor in the corner by the fish tank. A few minutes later my wife came into the kitchen holding the parts and asking what they were doing on the floor.

I said, "I told you I don't want the pieces from that nasty fish tank filter lying around in the kitchen!"

She replied, "Well, that's all well and good, Einstein, but these are the parts to the coffee pot!"

Oops! Not willing to give up so easily, I retorted, "Well, if we owned a simple Mr. Coffee like everyone else, instead of that high-tech coffee maker contraption which requires a degree in engineering to use, I might be able to tell the difference between coffeepot parts and fish tank filter parts!"

She simply shook her head and said, "Honey, one of these days you are going to *have* to learn about the new way things are being done in this technical world we live in."

"No way," I snapped. "I'm too old. I don't have the energy, and if this world has left me behind, so be it!"

The story makes a valid point, relative to leadership. You see, a middle-aged husband who hates both the fish tank filter parts and the coffeepot can throw a temper tantrum and refuse to learn new things. Leaders can't.

Leadership takes energy. It takes focus, concentration, and continual attention to the millions of details generated by the workplace. Because of the level of intensity required, it is easy for leaders to forget that there are other leaders out there facing the same questions, attempting to solve the same problems, and dealing with the same issues as those right at home. Re-training accomplishes two things: (1) it forces you to take a break—to get out of the office, get a fresh perspective, and renew your charge, and (2) it allows you to network with others who face similar challenges and frustrations, and to pick their brains about their approaches and experiences.

Without a doubt, it has been my experience that the benefits of continual re-training significantly outweigh the sacrifice of time away from the office. Not only have I returned with a renewed sense of energy, but I have met new colleagues and made friends along the way.

Be the lead dog...

- Don't hesitate to participate in some type of leadership training. The more you know going in, the better your chances for success.

- Regardless of the level of discomfort, try applying the new leadership knowledge you receive. If it works, keep it in place. If not, discard it and try something else.

- Take time out to get re-trained periodically. It will recharge your leadership battery and help you realize you are not in the leadership battle alone.

4

It's Not Good Enough To Aim—You Got to Hit!

◆

("Task-Centered" Leadership)

Arguments ensue relative to which style of leadership, "task-centered" or "people-centered", is most effective. When it's all said and done, most would simply conclude that some sort of balance is the best course of action. That being said, it is necessary to examine each to the extent that students of leadership at least recognize the elements of each style and attach the appropriate value in light of their own organization's expectations.

It was probably the Human Relations Movement that gave task-centered leadership a bad name and elevated the more touchy-feely leadership approach to a new level of popularity. In the same respect, it was the inappropriate actions of management over the years which led to the acceptance and bolstering of the labor unions. Even so, it does not mean that all managers are bad, nor that management is unnecessary. In the same respect, task-centered leadership may have gotten a bum rap, too.

Organizations are evaluated, in fact they live and die, on the basis of what they can accomplish. It is true that leaders must accomplish things through other people, but the bottom line is that they must get things *done*. It's not enough to occupy the corner office, dress well, attend meetings, and be nice to everyone. In the final analysis, the ultimate leadership question will be, "What have you accomplished?"

Success in this process is not achieved by a random, helter-skelter methodology. As with most meaningful pursuits, it follows a step-by-step process which begins with a concept and ends with the implementation of detailed plans. This process can be succinctly defined in five task-oriented leadership steps:

1. Develop a Plan

Whether you call it a plan, a vision, a goal, or a target, you must know where you are heading. Without an ultimate destination, your employees will be confused and frustrated. Decide what you want to accomplish, and then decide how you plan to get there.

2. Articulate the Plan

Once you've decided what to do, and how to do it, it might be a good idea to share it with those who are tasked to help you succeed. Too many leaders have great ideas, but expect their employees to consult Tarot cards to discover what they are thinking. Talk to your people. Set the direction, answer questions, and provide continual guidance.

3. Create Benchmarks

One of the most important things a task-oriented leader can do to increase the comfort level of his/her employees is to give them a way to measure their progress toward accomplishing the goal at hand. Some projects are simply too complex to wait until the end to determine progress. Employees like to know that they are on track and on target. Leaders who provide such information will find that the subordinates work harder and stay more focused if they have a "yardstick" available to them.

4. Establish a "Goal Line"

All good things must come to an end. Remember the goal is not the process…the goal is the end product. Imagine a football player carrying the ball, but never knowing where the goal line is. Employees are no different. If you are a task-oriented manager, it may be a bit difficult for you to declare a "finished product." Many task-oriented souls are never happy with the end result. They want to edit it, modify it, tweak it, change it, or re-work it. This is a battle you cannot win. Declare victory and move on.

5. Evaluate your Process and Product

Take an honest look at what you accomplished, and how well your team worked from start to finish. If there are ways to improve your process, now is the time to identify them. Be constructive in your criticism, and sincere in your expressions of appreciation. Remember that your success as a leader is only as good as your most recent accomplishment. A new task always looms in the near future.

Here are some task-oriented leadership questions you might want to ask yourself:

1. Do I know how to develop a vision for accomplishment?

2. How task-oriented am I as a person? Is getting the job done the most important thing to me?

3. Do I have the patience to allow others to help me, or do I jump in and take over at every turn?

4. What types of tangible measurement systems have I worked with, and what new benchmarking methodologies could I apply?

5. Can I remember working for a task-master? What did I enjoy or not enjoy about it?

6. Can I eventually be satisfied with an end product, or do I always want to do "one more thing" to it?

7. Can I stick with a project for the long term, or do I lose interest and want to go on to other things?

Task-oriented leaders can sometimes be intimidating, insensitive, and unapproachable. I worked for one some years back. He barked out orders, threatened the slower employees, criticized the work product, and seldom said, "thank you." But he got results. I'll always remember the things he accomplished through us. And I'll never forgive him for the way we were treated. I must admit, however, that task-oriented leaders clearly understand their role in organizational accomplishment. "People-centered" leadership is also important to the overall leadership mission, but the importance of task-orientation cannot be overlooked. When you hire a

fishing guide, you really don't care how s/he dresses, who built the boat, or what lake s/he chooses. The question is—can s/he find fish? When you look through task-oriented glasses, if s/he finds fish, s/he is successful. If not, s/he fails. The same can be said for leadership, and it often is.

Be the lead dog...

- Know that your leadership legacy is created just as much by what you accomplish as by how you treat people.

- Develop a plan, articulate the plan, measure the plan, complete the plan, and evaluate the plan. These steps will increase your chances for success.

- If you know that you are a task master, remember that your pups (subordinates) will respect you just as much, or more, if you scratch them behind the ears occasionally, instead of constantly kicking them in the rump.

5

Do I Look Like A People Person?

◆

("People-Centered" Leadership)

As we discussed in the last chapter, "task-centered" leadership focuses upon the leader's ability to accomplish a task or mission. "People-centered" leadership deals specifically with how the leader chooses, interacts with, and manages his/her human resources. I have already defended task-orientation as a purposeful part of the leadership formula. However, it is the people-centered skills which generally characterize a person as a good or bad leader. Every personality is different, and not everyone is going to be well-liked by all subordinates all of the time. But there are some general assumptions that can serve to assist you as you seek to hone your people-centered skills:

Assumption #1—Nobody likes a sourpuss

I've got an old tabby cat at home named Kitamiss who is the biggest killjoy of the feline world. I realize that most cats are a thankless lot anyway, but mine takes crabbiness to an art form. The terrier has been trying to make friends with her for the last six years, and all the dog has to show for it is a couple of whacks on the snout. The cat slinks around the house with a chip on her shoulder, hisses at anyone who attempts contact, and spends most of her time holed up in her cat condo. She's a far cry from a social butterfly. The thing of note here is that cats can get away with it, but leaders can't. Leaders are expected to interact with the people who work for them. They are expected to be friendly, up-beat, personable, and concerned for others. Leaders who are loners and spend most of their time behind a closed office door, will be quickly branded as insensitive and unconcerned. Contrary to popular belief, most people rather enjoy coming to work, like doing a good job, and value recognition and sincere expressions of appreciation from the boss. The leader who is negative, sees the glass as half-empty, and is quick to complain or ridicule will never be viewed as a people-person regardless of how s/he really feels inside.

Assumption #2—It doesn't cost anything to be polite.

Telling someone that they are wearing nice perfume is polite. Asking them how long they marinated in it is not. Peers and friends might be able to get away with cute little jabs and insults. Leaders can't do it. People know who the boss is. It isn't necessary to be demeaning, condescending, or mean to subordinates just to confirm it. If you are in charge, it is easy to make jokes about others. People will laugh because you're the boss and you told the joke, even if the joke isn't funny. But people file those things away. They don't forget, and they seldom forgive, if you embarrass them in front of other people. Further, "please" and "thank you" go a long way when you are attempting to accomplish things through others. Praising publicly and criticizing privately are just as important now as they always were. Constantly barking out orders and making unreasonable demands may work just because you are the boss, but it's a poor way to treat people, and it equates to lousy leadership.

Assumption #3—People aren't perfect. Don't expect them to be.

Ask a child, "Do you understand?" If s/he does, s/he will say, "yes." If not, s/he will say, "no." Ask an adult the same exact question and s/he will almost always answer in the affirmative. Because of this tendency, we spend a good deal of time in Instructor Techniques classes harping on the fact that adult students, because of ego, self-esteem, or arrogance, will say they understand when, in fact, they do not. Subordinates are the same way. Even your best employees are going to screw up from time to time. How you react is demonstrative of your skills as a people-centered leader.

I once told my administrative assistant, Nancy, to mail fifty certificates of completion to participants in a training course. The 8 x 11 certificates were very attractive, printed by the sponsoring agency, and signed by me, the supervisor, and the instructor. Nancy was not at her desk when I left the office, so I wrote her a note including the instruction which read, "Fold these as little as possible." When I got back, what do you think I found? Yep. fifty certificates, each folded five times each. She had done exactly what I told her to do, but not what I wanted her to do. Regardless of whether my instructions to her were poor, or she simply misunderstood, the fact is that appropriate communication did not occur. The certificates were ruined, and I had to deal with a "people-centered" leadership issue. "Perspective" becomes a critical factor when reacting to employee mistakes. I have a good friend and a great leader who swears by the adage that "no issue is worth damaging a relationship." I'm not sure I'm willing to go quite that far, but I do believe that much more harm can be done by inappropriately handling a subordinate error than was ever caused by the initial mistake. It was necessary to call Nancy's attention to the error, but it wasn't necessary to take her out and shoot her. Further, it was necessary for me to realize that I was to blame in part because of my misleading instructions. When deciding where to place the blame, it is sometimes good to also look in your own direction.

Assumption #4—Teamwork is a great concept

When I was in Junior High School we always chose up teams during gym class. Whether it was softball, football, or basketball, there were always a few of the less athletically talented students who were never chosen. We insensitively referred to them as the "leftovers." It was a very poor practice which was devastating to the egos of those never picked for a team. You can't help but wonder if they ever were fortunate enough later on to find out what it meant to really be part of a team. People like to be included. They like to know that they are a member of a group with everyone all pulling in the same direction to accomplish something meaningful. Leaders are instrumental in setting this tone for employees. In a sense, the leader becomes coach, cheerleader, referee, and score keeper for everything his/her employees do. It is a great concept for the people-centered leader. It compels employees to keep pace with the dictates of the project, and enjoins the group to pull together in times of crisis. The only imperative is that the leader pay close attention to ensure that no one is excluded and banished to the "leftovers." It can be a daunting task at times because subordinate talent levels vary greatly. Effective leaders attempt to recognize individual talents and focus them in a direction which maximizes employee involvement while looking for ways to help each employee improve his or her skills.

Assumption #5—People want to be led

There's an adult learning concept called "self-direction." It means that adults, even in learning situations, still desire to maintain some type of control over their lives. That concept transitions into the workplace as well, but it does not mean that people don't want to be led. Good leaders spend as much time looking back as they do looking forward. People are not sheep, but they do have an appreciation for someone who understands the mission, provides clear direction, and is willing to step out and "call the cadence" to keep everyone in step with one another. Employees who respect their leader, and feel confident in his/her ability to take them forward, are happier and more motivated to work. People like a leader with the confidence to shout, "follow me," provided that person has a plan and a purpose, and has demonstrated that s/he knows which direction to go.

Be the lead dog...

- Happiness is contagious. Leaders who are happy, friendly and polite will generally find that their subordinates engage in similar behavior.

- Employees are not machines, and they will err from time to time. Good leaders correct the behavior, but in such a way that the employee's self-esteem remains intact.

- Don't hesitate to take charge. You will be surprised at how people will be quick to follow your lead.

6

On Your Mark, Get Set, Splat!

♦

(Dealing With Leadership Failures)

The first words (and close to the last) uttered by General George Custer upon spotting the Indians at Little Big Horn were, "Hooray, fellas, we've got 'em now!" Failure is a fact of life. There are hundreds of clichés which exemplify that fact, e.g., "failure is more interesting than success," "woe to him who is alone when he falleth, "things started timidly fail with a boldness," "there is benefit to failing early in life" and so on and so on. Even excellent leaders fail from time to time. Failure isn't fun, but, with few exceptions, it is a recoverable condition. If there is a benefit to failure, it is at least the discovery of one more thing that will not work. But there are several irrefutable facts about failure that every timid leadership candidate should consider. Clearly, a ship is safer in the harbor than upon the sea, but that's not the reason ships get built. And leaders who fail to act out of fear of failure miss opportunities for action, growth, and potential greatness.

Fact #1 Leaders who do nothing seldom fail

Leadership can be a risky business. It involves juggling operational, strategic, political, and visionary balls, while trying not to drop any of them. In fact, the leader is very much like the street entertainer who juggles a bowling ball, a chain saw, a marshmallow, and a bowling pin. Every problem is weighted differently, and every challenge requires a unique approach. So based upon that, one might draw the superficial conclusion that leaders who don't take chances, don't do anything outside the box, and take a paycheck without ever straying from the "yellow brick road" will never be branded as failures. But that conclusion is flawed. A leader who never does anything will *not* be remembered as someone who never failed. S/he will instead be remembered as a "do nothing" who had numerous chances to shine, but always feared to embrace the unknown. History sanitizes a person. Some of the most revered leaders in history stumbled and fell flat on their faces, but in time came to be regarded as leadership examples. People love to forgive and, in most cases, will forget when a leader lays an egg or takes one on the chin. A professional baseball player with a batting average of .400 is considered to be a superstar hitter. But that means he's failing 60% of the times he's at bat. Leaders who act, fail, then brush themselves off and act again, are much more destined for success than the leader who buries his/her talents for fear of loss. Leaders who keep trying eventually succeed. The old adage that "even a blind pig finds an acorn once in a while" is applicable here. The implication is that the blind pig keeps trying. So should the person in a leadership position.

Fact #2 Failure is a part of the learning process…if you allow it

Snow skiing and I just don't get along. My wife introduced me to the sport one winter at the Copper Mountain Ski Resort in Colorado. Being a rather athletic guy, I assumed that snow skiing would simply be another of those sports that I would master in pretty short order. Not so. I flunked "bunny school" because I couldn't get the hang of turning. A number of small saplings gave up the ghost when I rammed into them while trying to stop. Flocks of skiers actually followed me down the slopes just to see which way I would fall next. I got snow inside my ski bibs in places where Sears promised snow could not get. In short, my first attempt at snow skiing was a complete, total failure. My wife, who is a rather accomplished skier, found the whole

thing to be somewhat humorous, but I was frustrated, embarrassed, and just about willing to chalk the whole abysmal trip off as a waste of time. But I didn't. I went to the ski lodge and pouted for a while, but then decided that giving up was just not my style. So I went back out, found a small slope, and with the help of my wife began to practice the basic moves required to negotiate the "green" runs. I must admit that now some years later I am still a Bozo when I don a pair of snow skis. And I will never be anything but a mediocre snow skier. But I feel a good deal better about the whole snow skiing experience than I would have had I not used the first few failures as an opportunity to learn.

Leadership is a "stepping stone" learning process. The longer you do it, the more you learn, and the better you get at it. As I always tell my students about my management years, "I may not have done too many things right, but I sure made enough mistakes along the way to know how *not* to do it." Sometimes that is the key. Falling is not failure, unless it is accompanied by a lack of desire to get back up. Learning from failure has great application to future success, providing failure is not seen as condemnation, but as a need to readjust and try again.

Fact #3 Failure is cushioned by strong relationships

Good leaders forge strong relationships with mentors, peers, and even subordinates. These relationships are never more meaningful to a leader than during times of failure. There is no more lonely a feeling than that of failing alone. Support systems exist for the exclusive function of propping us up until we can stand on our own once again. But those systems must be in place before the failure occurs.

I worked for a law enforcement executive who spent, in my opinion, far too much time catering to the local African-American ministerial alliance in our city. He went to breakfast meetings with them periodically, celebrated in their churches, donated to their causes, and conversed with them regularly on an individual basis. I questioned him about this one day and he simply replied that, "…you form interpersonal relationships before crisis occurs, not afterward." That lesson came home to roost some months later when one of our law enforcement officers accidentally and fatally shot an innocent juvenile member of the city's African-American community. Instead of raising arms and making threats, the ministers stood behind the Chief and the police department, certainly not condoning the action, but working together to prevent what could have easily deteriorated into an angry civil disturbance.

Everyone needs support from people around them who can share in successes, and also provide support during times of failure. The visionary leader knows that leadership is a "roller coaster" experience. It is exciting, and accompanied by continual ups and downs. But when the coaster hits the lowest point on the track, something must help it get back on top. Strong relationships built on friendship, integrity, and professionalism meet that need.

Fact #4 Failure must not only be faced, but embraced

Failure is understandable. Unwillingness to stand accountable for it is unacceptable. When my youngest daughter was twelve, she washed her cell phone. More precisely, she washed her jeans, the front pocket of which contained her cell phone, which should have been in her charger, but wasn't. The result was an extremely clean, good smelling cell phone, which no longer worked. When I grilled her about it, her response, as you might guess, was, "I don't know how the phone got there. It was in my charger the last time I saw it." Now you might expect a "laamo" excuse like that from an absent-minded pre-teen, but not from a person in a leadership position. And yet the motto of some managerial practitioners seems to be, "It's not whether you win or lose, but how you place the blame." It didn't take me long as a kid to realize that when my dad confronted me as to whether or not I was responsible for a wrong act, that he already knew the answer. The whole point of his questioning was to help him determine how many times he was going to apply the board of education to my seat of higher learning. Whether out of fear or just plain logic, I learned very quickly that to come clean in the very beginning was in my and my backside's, best interest.

When a leader fails, s/he seldom does so in a vacuum. There are usually plenty of witnesses who are not just interested in the failure, but in the manner in which the leader will stand accountable. If the leader admits error, and makes an honest, noble attempt not to repeat it, the whole issue quickly slips from the spotlight. If not, the occasion will be remembered and repeated ad nauseam, which serves up nothing positive for the organization or its leadership.

Fact #5 Failure is not generally fatal

As I stated earlier, failing is not fun. But in most situations it is not fatal either. Even though NASA's shuttle program has experienced two separate shuttle tragedies, the program continues to exist, and at a higher level of safety awareness than ever before. The early explorers faced peril on regular occasion, and made numerous mistakes in finding and identifying new lands. In some instances, they died in the process of interacting with strange and hostile cultures. But the idea of exploration never even slowed down. George Bush (not Dubya) wanted to be President of the United States, but he failed in his bid to secure the Republican nomination. It was won by Ronald Reagan, who went on to be President. But George Bush's failure was not complete. It took him an additional eight years of service as Reagan's Vice President before he finally realized his dream. His inability to secure the nomination against a very popular Ronald Reagan could be viewed as a failure on Bush's part. But it was not. As you know, he eventually achieved his goal of becoming president. So it is with leadership. There are no guarantees. But leaders who possess the right attitude, accompanied with a modicum of talent, can almost always prevent a failure from turning into a terminal incident.

Be the lead dog...

- Don't use the potential for failure as a reason not to act. Leaders are defined by what they do, not how safe they play it. Making mistakes is a part of the leadership process. Turn failure into a learning experience.

- Make some friends along the way. You may need them when times are tough.

- Remember that the easiest targets are those who are standing still. Keep zigzagging and you will successfully reach the finish line.

7

Seeing Beyond Your Nose

✦

(The Art of Leadership "Visioning")

Genius is not a prerequisite to leadership. But good leadership does require that a person be curious and persistent, with a willingness to think outside of established paradigms, and a penchant for exploring new ways of doing things. Significant lip service has been devoted to the concept of "visioning." For many, it has almost become a trite expression. But the ability to look at the overall picture of the organization and to evaluate it, modify it, and change it, is a primary responsibility of the effective organizational leader.

A friend of mine bought a retirement cabin in western North Carolina some years back. A good-sized, fast moving stream ran the entire length of his property. He noticed that the creek bed was lined with some rather large, smooth stones which were both wet and covered with a type of moss which made them treacherously slippery if one tried to wade across the stream. Still in all, every time he looked at the individual stones, he envisioned a wall in front of his cabin. Finally, one day he began to remove the stones, one at a time, and to clean and dry them in the sun. Eventually, he collected hundreds of stones and pieced them together to form a strong, sturdy, attractive wall in front of his house. It's a simple example but it proves a point. The slippery wet stones in the bottom of his creek would still be slippery wet stones had he not seen a wall in his mind's eye beforehand.

That's all visioning is. It is the ability to look at a bunch of individual parts and see something greater than their sum. It is the process of examining the way things are accomplished, and considering if there might not be a new way to skin the cat. It is the willingness to view a procedure from a different perspective and wonder if an additional purpose could be equally served.

Good leaders don't always know the answers, but they never quit asking questions. They understand that although they may find nothing really new, there is always a need to keep the old fresh. And they are not satisfied with the status quo, even though the status quo might seem to be working satisfactorily.

During my research for this book, I had the opportunity to converse with a number of intelligent professional colleagues and good friends. One serves as the pastor of a small church in one of our local communities. Some of the members of his congregation became concerned that when he completed his doctorate, he might move on to pastor a larger church in another area. In fact, he *had* been approached with a number of other offers. I queried him about this situation during one of our conversations, and, in essence, this is what he said:

"Yes, I am aware of their concerns, and a move of some type is not totally out of the question. But the attainment of my doctorate really has nothing to do with it. I have a vision for this small church. I have considered it at length, and prayed for guidance about the direction in which I should lead it. I have a clear picture of where I think we need to go, and a pretty well-defined time line relative to when we ought to get there. That is my vision as their pastor, their leader. In time, I will reveal this vision to them. Then they must decide if they will fall into step with me to help it become a reality. This is my passion. They may decide that my vision is not their vision. That is what will determine my length of service with this church. If I cannot get them to buy into my leadership vision, then my work here is done, and I will move on."

So one might ask, "Why would a congregation so devoted to their pastor not want to follow his direction as their leader?" The answer to that question is summed up in the fact that overcoming conventional wisdom is never easy. For centuries people believed that Aristotle was right when he said that the heavier an object, the faster it would fall to earth. Aristotle was regarded as the greatest thinker of all time and surely he could not be wrong. All it would have taken was for one brave person to take two objects, one heavy and one light, and drop them from a great height to see whether or not the heavier object landed first. But no one stepped forward until nearly 2000 years after Aristotle's death. In 1589, Galileo summoned learned professors to the base of the leaning Tower of Pisa. Then he went to the top and pushed off a ten-pound and a one-pound weight. Both landed at the same time. But the power of belief in the conventional wisdom was so strong that the professors denied what they had seen. They continued to say Aristotle was right.

That is why a leader's vision must be his/her passion. Vision is not a snapshot made up of impulsive thoughts and fluff, but rather a creative mental invention of something between a thought and a thing created from hours of layered focus and concentration. It takes a great deal of management energy and enthusiasm, and requires a persistent desire to sell it to those who are resistant to change.

Persistence is an integral part of making something real out of a creative idea. Good leaders develop it early in their careers, and employ it constantly. A young man made an appointment for an interview with a prestigious corporation. He asked if he could get into their well-respected management trainee program. The very busy personnel manager, besieged with applications, said, "Impossible now. Come back in about ten years." The applicant responded, "Would morning or afternoon be better?" This young man understood the importance of persistence and determination from the very beginning. In the same manner, the leader's ability to gain acceptance of a new idea must be fortified by a similar form of perseverance.

Generally, people don't like change. Even if the change is for the better, it is traumatic. Most subordinates would usually prefer to amble along in the same manner rather than suffer through the rigors of change. For that reason, it pays for the persistent leader to use good timing and charismatic salesmanship when introducing his/her plans for change. If the vision is simply dropped into subordinates' laps without the benefit of introduction and systematic explanation, it's like tossing the employee into a swimming pool in the middle of February. Introducing change is a bit like training a gorilla to walk on a leash. It may be possible, but it can be particularly difficult and it annoys the heck out of the gorilla.

Therein lies the leadership challenge. "Bear" Bryant was arguably the finest college football coach who ever lived. The records he set and the legacy he left is still talked about today, many years after his death. But regardless of his football knowledge, and despite the hundreds and hundreds of pep talks he delivered to his players, his motto contained only four words. As long as he coached, he kept a sign hanging on his locker room door. It simply read "Cause Something To Happen." Good leaders are not in the organizational ocean to test the waters. They are in it to make waves.

There's an old adage that says, "It's not what you know that counts, it's what you think of—in time." Throughout my career I have watched many professional managers strive and struggle to attain leadership positions. They spent years with their noses to the grindstone, and their ears to the political rail so that one day they might reach a point on the organizational ladder where their creative ideas could really make a difference. Yet when they finally attained that high rung, they stopped and spent the rest of their time admiring the view, forgetting what their initial reason was for wanting to climb. Leadership is measured not by the rank one attains in the organization, but by what s/he does with that rank. Developing a creative vision is not the be-all and end-all of the leader's job, but it is a very definite and important piece of the pie.

Be the lead dog...

- Curiosity may kill cats, but it inspires leaders. Never quit looking for something new.

- Always keep things moving. Motionless organizations become stagnant.

- Persistence pays. Work to sell your ideas to others.

- Remember that change is sometimes difficult for subordinates. Cushion your persistence with patience and politeness.

8

Pulling A Rabbit Out Of A Hat

◆

(Solving Unusual Leadership Problems)

One night, after several long hours of work at home, I opened a beer and stepped out onto my front porch. The hour was late, the weather was brisk, and a full moon lit up the front yard. I sat down on the stoop, took a drink, and looked up to find the biggest, blackest jack rabbit I had ever seen sitting on its hind legs, staring at me from about fifteen feet away. I closed my eyes, shook my head, and immediately considered swearing off  beer. I stood up, went back inside, and woke my wife. "Come here. I need you to see something."

She was less than enthusiastic. "Leave me alone. I'm sleeping."

"No, get up. This will only take a second."

I dragged her to the front door, opened it, pointed to the rabbit, and said, "What is that?"

"It's a black rabbit," she annoyingly replied.

"Thank you. You can go back to sleep now." The rabbit hadn't moved, and seemed in no hurry to go anywhere. I went to the refrigerator and got a carrot. Once outside, I broke the carrot in half and tossed a piece over to him. He dropped down on all fours, hopped past the carrot, and stopped right beside my foot. Knowing next to nothing about rabbits, but sensing no real danger, I reached down, stroked his head a couple of times, and gave him the piece of carrot I still had in my hand. He took it, sat upright again, and began to munch. Within a few minutes, I came to realize that this was someone's pet who had escaped the confinement of his pen. I carefully picked him up, took him around to the garage, and gave him a safe haven until morning. The next morning, I saw a couple of neighborhood kids roaming the yards and calling for Bugsy. Obviously this was not the first time Bugsy had decided to go A.W.O.L. and visit strange new places late at night. I rounded the kids up, took them to my garage, and happily reunited them with their naughty, wayward rabbit.

Now, you might ask, "What the heck does a rabbit story have to do with leadership?" The answer is "lots." At least when it comes to dealing with unusual situations. All leaders face decisions on a daily basis which are algorithmic. That is to say they are repetitive, well-understood, and decided in the same way every time they are encountered. Filling out routine forms, granting employee requests, and approving time sheets provide no unusual challenges for good managers. Occasionally however, a problem is encountered that, although not necessarily complex, is unusual. It is a situation that has never occurred before, and may never occur again. For that reason, it is non-programmed, and there is no familiar formula to follow for successfully dealing with it. It is during such times that good leaders shine. Although they may have never faced the situation before, they are able to craft an approach based upon a set of valid, creative criteria that eventually provides a path to a solution. It might be valuable to consider some of these criteria. Here are some ideas:

1. Look for similarities to things which have happened in the past. It is easy to get discouraged when faced with something for which there appears to be no quick solution. But, truth be known, there are very few *new* things in the universe. Most things are like other things in some way. Good leaders understand the concept of "transference." In other words, if you can take this new, unusual situation, and relate it to something which is already anchored, then it becomes more approachable, understandable, and solvable.

2. Seek the "obvious" first. Although this will probably not solve the problem, there is no need to make a problem harder than it is. Make sure an easy approach won't work before considering more difficult steps. Although it is not practical in times of crisis, there are occasions when simply allowing some time to pass helps make the unusual more understandable. Not every problem is a "hot button." Picking up the rabbit was not my first alternative. Although that is what I ended up doing, I was at first content to wait and see if he might hop away on his own, thereby eliminating my need for action.

3. Split the pie. Talented managers know better than to try to grasp the whole of the problem at one time. It is common knowledge that the digestive process works more efficiently with small bites rather than big ones. Many times, solving major problems is simply a process of making a sufficient number of smaller decisions as a means to an end.

4. Invent a new formula. Look at the situation from a different perspective. Back your way into the answer. Brainstorm solutions. Make assumptions and suppositions. Ask, "What would happen if I did this?" In our decision-making classes, we use an exercise called, "The Bean Jar." It is a standard sized Mason jar which is filled to the brim with dried beans. There are no golf balls hidden in the middle, nor any other tricks to make it seem more than it is…just a jar full of beans. The job for the students is to determine how many beans are in the jar; not by simply guessing, but by creating a formula, applying that formula, and arriving at a total number of beans based upon some type of creative process. Two things always impress me. Initially, how close some of the students come to pinpointing the correct number of beans and secondly, the unique, unusual formulas they construct which actually work. Effective leaders do not run from unusual problems. In fact (just like my terrier) when they see trouble, they head right in that direction. If the traditional methods of skinning the cat seem ineffective, they confidently create new methods which many times work, and work well.

5. Seek counsel. I have discussed this in other chapters, but it bears repetition. There are always people inside your organization who know more about some things than you do. Talk to them, regardless of their formal position. See what they think. Pick their brain as to how *they* would approach the situation. Listen carefully as they express their thoughts. Interlace their ideas with yours to form a new, combined approach. A good leader does not let ego get in the way of reaching a successful conclusion. S/he uses every human resource which is available, and gives appropriate credit to those who help.

6. Use every one of the five senses which are applicable. Draw pictures and/or diagrams. Build models, create new research words, phrases, or ideas related to the problem. Discover ways to re-package old ideas and make them fresh. There are no limits to creativity. The more it is employed, the more the solutions become obvious.

7. Avoid discouragement. One of the thrills of leadership comes from seeking out new horizons, and conquering them with creative approaches inside the well-parametered confines of the organizational structure. Seldom are football coaches revered for the common boilerplate plays that all teams use. The real winners are the ones who step outside the box and continue to try new ways of doing things until something finally clicks, and clicks big.

**Be the lead dog...**

• Look at unusual situations as a chance to do something unique and memorable. There is always a solution. Seek it out.

• Transfer the new problem to something similar which may have happened in the past. Seldom are unusual situations so different that they cannot be related to something known.

• Break the not-so-obvious down into smaller, more obvious pieces. Unusual situations are less unusual when you take them a step at a time.

• Don't try to do everything by yourself. Others are eager to help if you seek them out.

9

It's Hard to Look Cool When You Forget Your Pants

◆

(Making Silly Leadership Mistakes)

It has been my good fortune to manage many excellent people throughout my career. It has been a joy to watch them grow and develop. For the most part, they became successful leaders, and seldom experienced too many of the failures I wrote about in chapter six. But that doesn't mean they didn't bungle things from time to time. For that reason I talked with numerous subordinates who related some of the silly mistakes their leaders have made. As a result, it became obvious to me that good leaders must not only be on the lookout for major problems that might result in cataclysmic failure, but also for the commonplace day-to-day mud puddles which, if not negotiated properly, make the leader look a bit silly.

Pitfall #1 Failure to see that which is readily apparent

When I was a young police officer on the street, I was sent by headquarters to serve a witness subpoena. I stepped onto the porch of the house and rang the doorbell. Through the open window, I could see a pre-teen boy who was struggling while practicing repetitive scales on the piano. Upon hearing the doorbell, the young pianist got up and answered the door. I asked the boy, "Young man, is your mother home?" The kid looked at me with a smirk on his face and said, "Duh! Now, what do *you* think?" To be sure, some of the problems of leadership are incredibly difficult. They can be like a 1000 piece jigsaw puzzle demanding hours of stressful concentration to resolve. But that doesn't mean that we should skip common sense decisions and move right to the more difficult options. Sometimes the answer to the problem is right under our nose if we could quit looking at the forest long enough to focus on the trees. There's a story about a woman who came home to find her husband in the kitchen, shaking frantically with what looked like a wire running from his waist towards the electric kettle. Intending to jolt him away from the deadly current, she grabbed the kitchen mop and whacked him as hard as she could with the metal handle, breaking his arm in two places. Until that moment the poor guy had been happily listening and dancing to his Walkman. Training and intellect are two very important tools for the leader. But so is common sense. It's why we ask people "Can you breathe?" before automatically beginning mouth-to-mouth resuscitation. Look first to the obvious. It may save you significant trouble and embarrassment.

Pitfall #2 Failure to remain modest

Self-confidence is a blessing. Overconfidence can be a curse. Leaders who are overconfident tend to make impulsive decisions which are not always characterized by good judgment. Overconfidence is generally caused by a lack of experience and fixes itself in time, provided the person does not make a critical error early in the learning process. This is not so much an intellectual problem as it is a "sawing before measuring" mentality.

In the public safety organization where I worked, the management philosophy was to transfer managers every two to four years into a different management arena. The premise was that this produced, in the long run, a better-rounded, more competent manager. For the most part, I experienced few problems with my assignments, until one year when I was transferred to the Drug Unit. Of all the areas in which I had worked, the Drug Enforcement Division was one about which I knew very little.

I read some books, asked around, and discovered that the science of drug investigation was difficult, dangerous, and definitely a challenge to manage. Fortunately, I had enough common sense to realize it would take some time to develop the necessary expertise. So on the first night of my new assignment, I called a meeting with all of my subordinates. I explained to them that I had several years of management experience, and was looking forward to working with them. Unfortunately, since I didn't know the difference between a marijuana tablet and a cocaine cigarette, they would have to help me learn. And they did. Within a few months I had grasped enough knowledge to begin effectively leading this group of enthusiastic personnel. Overconfidence can be interpreted as arrogance, and it interferes with supervisor/subordinate relationships. If you don't know, better to admit it and ask for help. People are happy to lend a hand as long as you don't appear to be a know-it-all.

Pitfall #3 Failure to remember that leaders *need* followers

Without a team there is no need for the coach. Without students there is no need for the teacher. Without teachers there is no need for the principal. And on it goes. Occasionally, the leader needs to look back and make sure s/he still has some followers. The manager/subordinate relationship is not a master/slave existence. Without motivated, dedicated subordinates, managers will get little accomplished. Subordinates want to be led, but they also like to be a part of the process. Good leaders present the challenge, encourage employees during the application process, and frequently evaluate worker progress. Since no one is an expert in everything, good leaders surround themselves with people who make up for their deficiencies. In my years as a practitioner, I was quite cognizant of my weakness in handling analytical details. Policies, statistics, and budgets were neither my favorite tasks, nor my strong points. For that reason, I always kept an employee or two close by who not only liked that type of work, but was good enough at it to keep my fanny out of the fire.

Pitfall #4 Failure to delegate

All of us understand that a basic premise of leadership is to get things accomplished through subordinates. This translates into clearly describing the task to be accomplished, then allowing others to do the work within the parameters which have been established for the project. There is seldom a problem if the subordinates understand the mission, and are talented enough to proceed with a little direction and supervision. The rub comes when subordinates continually stumble and fumble their way along, thereby prompting the leader to jump in and take over the day-to-day details in order to keep the project on track. Part of a leader's job is to teach. Unfortunately this means allowing subordinates the leeway to make mistakes and to learn by doing. The leader who is too quick to wrest the process from workers who are not as astute or as efficient as the leader would like, does the subordinate and the organization a disservice. Not all workers catch on at the same rate. Some are quick studies, while others may never rise to a level of excellence. But the effective leader struggles to ensure that all the workers under his/her supervision have the opportunity to perform at their best level, while offering support and guidance without retaking possession of the project.

Pitfall #5 Failure to follow up

Nothing is more exciting than the announcement and initiation of a new project. In some respects, we are like a child with a new toy and we focus all of our energy and enthusiasm on its implementation. But like the morning dew, the enthusiasm and energy soon diminish, and all that remains is the tedious work required to bring the project to fruition. To be sure, a good leader is responsible for setting the stage and motivating his/her employees to get a new task rolling. But the responsibility for step-by-step review and follow-up is even more important. The leader who relishes the moment when the project jumps out of the blocks, but fails to hang tough during the hard, long months of development and trial, reminds me of the politician who arrives at a public hearing and announces his purpose for being there as one of "listening" and "learning," then sneaks out an hour later to attend a Burger King opening. It's a pretty easy formula...fanfare without follow-up equals eventual failure.

Pitfall #6 Failure to stay on top of your game

Good leaders revel in accomplishment. They develop reputations for success, and rightly so. But, too often, some leaders become content to drift along, eventually deteriorating into mediocre managers who are content to rest upon the successes of yesterday's projects, with no real desire to keep their edge sharp. Good leaders remember that they are only as good as they continue to make themselves. They constantly ask questions such as, What else can I learn?, How can I improve relationships?, What are others doing that I can emulate?, How can I improve the way we do business?, and How can I enhance my personal leadership style? I see too many managers who haven't been to a training seminar in years. They don't feel that they need it because they have already attained management status. And their management style exhibits that mentality. They are about as interesting as a day old doughnut.

Pitfall#7 Failure to think strategically

In some respects this amplifies pitfall #5, but takes it a step further. Most successful accomplishments begin with a broad brush concept or a feeling for what is to be accomplished. This is important. Everyone who is involved needs to know where the project starts and what the ultimate goal will be. But the devil is always in the details. Good leaders must be willing to roll up their sleeves and get their hands a little dirty by thinking strategically about how to get from one point to the other. As I write this, we are presently in the process of constructing a new instructional facility at the college. Upon its completion, it will be a multi-million dollar state of the art teaching facility. From its inception, I have been impressed with the concern of the leaders to stay on time, under budget, and allow no compromises in quality or efficiency. They successfully accomplish this by following a well-developed strategic plan which was created before the first shovel of dirt was turned. As the project has developed, it has been necessary to deviate from the original plan, but when this occurs, everyone in charge is aware of such action, and documents it as a concrete construction decision, rather than a by-the-seat-of-the-pants guess. Concepts are great, but they are not enough. Good leaders invest the time early on to construct a "road map" which will ensure that efforts remain efficient, effective, and on target.

Pitfall #8 Failure to admit ignorance

No one knows all there is to know about everything. One of the painful lessons I learned early on as an instructor was that there is always someone in the classroom who knows more about a particular subject than I do as the instructor. That seldom causes a problem unless I, as an instructor, purport to know things I really don't know. Many years ago I taught a stress management class to a group of state criminal justice employees in Tallahassee, Florida. I knew little about their backgrounds, and frankly was uninterested. While writing a chemical compound on the board, I forgot the letter and number sequence for one of the formulas. Telling myself that none of the students would know anyway, I simply substituted another compound into the formula and went on to make my point. When I received my evaluations at the end of the day I was shocked to learn that I had been teaching a classroom full of forensic scientists who knew the minute I wrote the formula on the board that it was wrong. They were irritated that I had assumed their ignorance, and I paid for it on the evaluations. Rectification of this error is simple. Good leaders, who don't know, say so. Then they find out, or they seek outside sources that can help. There is no shame in not knowing...only in not knowing and failing to admit it.

Be the lead dog...

- Work the simple solutions first. Don't make things harder than they are.

- Be confident, but don't trip over your ego.

- Always remember the people who work for you. They help make you what you are.

- Help your people do the work. Don't do it for them.

- Follow-up isn't fun, but it is necessary. Do it.

- Stay sharp. There is always something else to learn.

- Winning is a step-by-step process. Get a game plan before you begin.

- Don't be afraid to admit you don't know. Others stand ready to help you.

10

"My Fellow Americans…"

♦

(The Leader's Role as Figurehead)

Rudolph Giuliani was not always the most popular mayor of New York City. He used an aggressive political style, and had a tendency to be blunt and insensitive when dealing with others. But when the tragic circumstances of 9-1-1 occurred, he promptly switched gears, donned his jacket and New York City Police cap, and walked the streets of New York offering support and calming fears for days on end. The result was obvious. His popularity soared, his reputation became international, and he is today regarded as one of the great heroes in the aftermath of that horrific event.

The role of "figurehead" is a leadership responsibility which cannot be denied. Even if the leader is shy, uncomfortable, or even disinterested in this particular responsibility, s/he must recognize that this role is key to both the organization's image and success. In many respects, it is the symbol of management's concern for employees, customers, and the community it serves.

Fortunately, it does not always emanate from tragedy. Most of the time, more good things happen than bad. But this also offers the leader a chance to be on stage. During the entire time that I served in public safety, my organization scheduled regular "award ceremonies" where we celebrated promotions, project successes, and contributions made by employees both inside and outside the organization. These ceremonies were always well-attended, and those who were to receive recognition frequently invited family and friends to celebrate their good fortune. At the end of the celebration, the leader of the organization was always called upon to offer some words of encouragement and motivation to those in attendance. If s/he did it right, everyone walked away with a warm, fuzzy feeling about both the leader and the organization. That is as it should be. To be sure, leaders must ensure that the organization is effective, efficient, and profitable. Without these things, the organization soon ceases to exist. In light of this, the role of figurehead may seem the most basic and simple of management roles. But employees do not want to follow a ghost. They want their leader to be visible, articulate, friendly, and charismatic. And they quickly become disenchanted if they do not observe these qualities.

Here at the college, we participate in a huge graduation ceremony approximately every eight to ten weeks. For those of us in leadership positions, it is often the same old thing with the same old speeches, the same old awards, and the same old chicken wings at the reception. For us it gets extremely old. But we continually remind ourselves that for the new recruit who has just successfully completed a difficult and comprehensive course of study, it is a magical night. If we, as leaders, demonstrate a lack of enthusiasm for their achievement, it is obvious and disappointing to each of the graduates, and diminishes our credibility as leaders.

The ascension to leadership automatically carries with it the role of figurehead. As such, there exists a number of functions that the leader must embrace. Each is unique and important to those in the organization.

1. Information dissemination. Information has always been, and will continue to be, the lifeline of the organization. Although the grapevine exists, and is very powerful, most surveyed employees indicate that they would prefer to hear important information, both good and bad, directly from the organizational leaders. The reality for management is that this practice can be time-consuming, unproductive, and the genesis of complaint sessions with employees. Nonetheless, good leaders take advantage of opportunities to share information with others. This creates the impression of candor, openness, and concern among subordinates. Obviously some information exists which cannot be shared with everyone in the organization. However, the leader's willingness to impart information which *can* be shared, paints the picture of a leader who has confidence in his/her employees and has nothing to hide.

2. Organizational spokesperson. Organizations do not exist in a vacuum. They are often required to take an official position, and to speak in support of that position. Because of the increasing demands of the press and the public, many organizations have created public information positions in order to handle the information dissemination function. This is fine for most day-to-day interrogatories. But there are times when only the organizational leader will do. People see the chief executive and the organization as one. How the executive presents the organization's case, responds to questions from the media, and controls his/her emotions is critical to whether the position is accepted or rejected. Unfortunately, many of those desiring information, especially the media, can be cruel and insensitive in their pursuit. Such is the burden of being a spokesperson. The more often a leader assumes this role, the better s/he gets at it; but a primary premise is to be as honest as possible, and recognize that others outside the organization have a legitimate interest in the organization's actions.

3. External liaison. In some respects, interest in the actions of an organization actually stretches beyond that of curiosity. In many instances, external pressures bear upon organizational leaders to allow persons outside the immediate organization to participate in the decision-making processes. CEOs are constantly required to interact with board directors, competitors, and lenders to ensure continued progress without interference. There is not a public safety executive alive who has not had to deal with commissioners and special interest groups who want to influence promotions, interagency transfers, and organizational policy decisions. Unfortunately, leaders cannot simply ignore these "flies in the ointment." They have a duty to work with those who may have a legitimate right to be involved, and even with those who do not, but possess enough power to wiggle themselves into the process. The role of external liaison is not just one of cooperation and communication. It is one of organizational promotion and protection. Uncomfortable as this responsibility may be, it falls squarely on the shoulders of the leader.

Some leaders find the role of organizational figurehead to be a task which is of little interest or importance. However, employees, customers, and other interested parties are seldom pleased if the leader passes this role off to someone else. During good times, and most especially bad times, the leader who plays the role of figurehead effectively can provide support, encouragement, and hope for those who show up daily to get the job done.

Be the lead dog...

- When it comes to the role of "figurehead," the organization and the leader are viewed by others as a single entity.

- Good leaders work to keep their image fresh, even though the process is boring and repetitive.

- Organizations are not islands. A major responsibility of the leader is to develop liaisons with everyone necessary in an effort to get ahead and get along.

11

Up To Your Knees in Dishwashing Soap

✦

(Handling The Troubles of Leadership)

Leadership is not measured by how much trouble you can avoid. It is measured by how you handle the troubles you encounter. The successful leader is the one who can steer the organization in a positive direction, while successfully negotiating the mundane obstacles, both large and small, which would prevent success if not dealt with accordingly. This isn't accomplished in a random manner, but rather by a set of systematic steps which, although not always, allows the leader to move the barriers just enough to slide the organization forward. In talking with successful troubleshooting leaders, I have discovered five common methodologies which good leaders employ to successfully steer their organizational ship.

1. Work through your feelings before taking action. Although some problems are systemic, coincidental, and/or simply bad luck, most problems can be quickly traced back to someone who either did not do what they were tasked to do, or did not do it the correct way. Leaders are human beings. They can be happy, sad, and angry. There is nothing wrong with emotion. But reacting impulsively, especially when strong emotional feelings are involved, can sometimes damage relationships and even exacerbate the problem. One of the fascinating  things about our brain is that it enables us to process information very quickly.

Consequently, a good leader is able to frame a problem, examine it from different perspectives, consider alternatives, and determine a preliminary course toward a solution before ever saying a word. Another consideration is that it is difficult to be intellectual and emotional simultaneously. Allowing time for emotions to diminish will settle the situation, and enable the leader to focus upon the problem itself. Finally, the leader must determine if, in fact, s/he may have played a role in the creation of the problem. Statistics tell us that as much as 70% of all business communication is misunderstood. A leader who may have been part of the problem, and is willing to admit it, is much more highly respected than the one who looks to assign all of the blame to others.

2. Initiate the action. I was asking a colleague of mine what he respected the most about his boss, a reputably very effective leader. He replied that "every time she sees a potential problem, she gets excited." Problems which are ignored simply become more complex problems which take more time and energy to resolve. I hate going to the dentist. It is for that very reason that I try hard never to miss an appointment. I want to deal with any problems while they are small. I don't want to pay the price associated with ignoring proper dental care. To take the point a bit further, it is not only the leader's responsibility to solve problems quickly, but to actually be on the lookout for them. The old adage that "those who go looking for trouble usually find it" is also true of leadership. Defensive driving instructors have been preaching this for years. "Keep your eyes moving. Look out for the erratic movements of other drivers. Let aggressive drivers go by so you can keep them out front where you can see them. Be ready to take evasive action if necessary." The result is not always "accident free driving." But it significantly reduces the defensive driver's chances of ending up in a wreck.

In the late eighteenth century, pioneers (mostly from farming families) traveled from the Ohio River Valley west across the Great Plains by means of the Conestoga wagon. The vast distance through unsettled country and the danger from Native Americans made it necessary to travel in large parties. These people were unskilled fighters and inexperienced travelers and therefore hired wagon masters to lead them to their destination. These wagon masters were hired not just to accompany the wagon train, but to serve as military captains and to help the pioneers deal with the problems and hazards they encountered along the way. In many respects, the success or failure of the journey was dependent upon the talent and diligence of the wagon master. So it is with the organizational leader. S/he is charged with the responsibility of constant problem identification and determining a solution. Such responsibility is best accomplished by always taking the initiative at every problematic juncture.

3. Attack the action rather than the employee. One afternoon I loaded the dishwasher with a bunch of dirty dishes. Upon discovering that we were out of automatic dishwashing detergent, I just said "what the heck," and squirted in a cup of the liquid soap we used to hand wash dishes in the sink. I turned the machine on and left for a few minutes. When I came back, the entire kitchen floor was covered in soap bubbles, and the dishwasher was churning like Mount Vesuvius. Everybody does stupid things from time to time. It is part of learning, and a condition of being human. Empowered leaders understand that good employees already feel bad when they make a mistake. Fixing the blame may be a requirement, but fixing the blame does not fix the problem. How a leader goes about dealing with a problem is just as important as solving the problem itself. Yelling, screaming, browbeating, and berating an errant employee may make the boss feel better, but it seldom accomplishes anything meaningful, and it can ruin employer/employee relationships. Smart leaders ask three questions when a problem occurs: 1) what went wrong? 2) *why* did it go wrong? and 3) what can we do to prevent it in the future? Each is a legitimate question which seeks to focus on the action as opposed to the employee. Good leaders seek to solve the problem *and* salvage the employee. Employees who inadvertently do something which causes a problem, but then are allowed to assist in solving that problem, escape with their egos intact, and a high level of enthusiasm for avoiding future mistakes.

4. Seek cooperation and conciliation. Some problems are so complex, and some opinions so divergent, as to prevent the solution of a problem. Many times in congress we observe that all parties concerned understand the problem and wish to solve it. But they simply cannot come to consensus as to which action is most appropriate. I once had a boss who would never let issues interfere with relationships. I am not prepared to agree totally with his philosophy, but I do know that cooperation is an integral part of keeping the organization viable and productive. Many times throughout my career, I found myself in absolute disagreement with another manager about the appropriate approach to solving a problem. But I also knew that once this issue was resolved (and even if it wasn't), that person and I would *eventually* have to team up down the road to resolve another conflict. "Agreeing to disagree" may be the most success you ever achieve in some situations. But disagreeing without being disagreeable is always a higher road. For years I worked with a certain peer in my organization. I would get promoted and he would work for me, then he would get promoted and I would work for him, and so it went for twenty five years. We clashed intellectually on a number of issues, and, at times, were simply unable to reach consensus. But we never allowed our professional disagreements to deteriorate into personal attacks. In the final analysis we both forgot about the issues which seemed so important, but remained good friends even after retirement. Some have said that "cooperation and compromise" is a poor problem solving approach because nobody ever gets what they really want. But if a little of what you want is better than nothing at all, and relationships are preserved in the process, it is worth consideration by a smart leader.

5. Don't hesitate to ask for help. Don't think for one moment that I wasn't embarrassed about that dishwasher soap bubble problem. But it didn't take long for me to realize that the bubbles were already over my ankles and heading toward my knees. I knew I needed help and fast. So when I started yelling, family members came running (and laughing—see chapter nine) with towels, and buckets, and mops. Even the smartest leaders need help sometimes. If we attempt to do everything based upon an isolated thought process, we not only work harder, but we run the risk of missing the best solution to the problem. It has been my experience that almost everyone possesses unique and useful talents. And almost everyone is willing to share if I am willing to ask. Good leaders seek to form teams. They lead, to be sure, but they see value in the input of others, and encourage them to participate in solution identification. Organizations are social entities that find solidarity and success through the interaction of its members. Being the boss means being in charge. But it does not mean "knowing everything." Never hesitate to ask for help. Advice gives you an advantage, and as long as you give credit where it is due, you will seldom be forced to solve problems alone.

**Be the lead dog...**

- Think first, act second. Emotional interference prevents sound thinking and judgment.

- Don't ignore the problem. Initiate whatever action is necessary in a timely manner.

- Resolve the problem without ruining the employee.

- Preserve relationships if at all possible. Issues disappear. Peers don't.

- Get help if you need it. People love to give advice to the boss.

12

Driving Straight on a Twisted Highway

✦

(Leadership Integrity)

Mary and Bill, two middle managers, were having lunch. Mary was buying. The reason for the meeting was that Mary had recently been transferred to Bill's department. She had never worked for Bill's boss before, and she wanted to pick Bill's brain concerning her new manager's mannerisms and expectations. She was very frank with Bill about what she wanted, and he saw no harm in answering a few questions if it would help her adjust. Over lunch, she asked some very pointed questions about the boss, and Bill was confidentially candid. He told her that the boss in question could be difficult to work for, and was sometimes unreasonable in his demands. In response to Mary's specific question about his having an "eye" for the ladies, Bill mildly cautioned that the man did have somewhat of a reputation for a little too much touching, hugging, and flirting with women who worked for him. When lunch was over, Mary seemed genuinely appreciative of Bill's honesty and directness.

The next morning, Bill had a note in his box to see the boss as soon as he arrived. When he reported to the boss's office, he noticed that the door was ajar. Bill walked to the door and knocked quietly. When he did, he saw Mary sitting in the office. The boss told Bill to have a seat outside, and then he got up and shut the door. Bill assumed Mary was getting her new job instructions. Ten minutes later, the boss opened the door and Mary quickly walked out without acknowledging Bill. Bill watched her leave, and then looked back at the boss, who motioned for Bill to come in and shut the door. There was no offer for Bill to sit down. The boss sat down at his desk, shuffled a paper or two, and then, without looking up, said, "So, I hear you've been running around telling everybody that I'm an unreasonable bully who likes to put the moves on the women." All of a sudden Bill felt like he'd just been kicked in the gut.

Integrity, in some respects, is a tough concept to grasp. The word itself is easy enough to understand. It involves the firm adherence to a code of values. But for some reason it gets corrupted inside the organization. Due to politics, competition for position, resources and/or market share, its definition gets blurred, and its application becomes situational. It's pretty clear here that our friend Bill had been set up. For whatever her reason, by violating Bill's confidence, Mary betrayed a trust and compromised her integrity. People like this will probably always exist in the organization. But for the organizational leader, integrity is imperative in every instance. It is almost imperative that the higher one goes, the more careful s/he must be to act in a manner which is above reproach. Perhaps Bill should have remained silent about the boss's womanizing habits, but the fact is that the boss shouldn't have been doing it in the first place. Leaders live in a fish bowl where every action they take is observed, examined, and discussed around the water cooler. Although the leader can do little to stop the gossip, s/he is obligated to exhibit behavior which is always above reproach.

If a person has reached a level of management, and has done so legitimately, then s/he is already doing some things right. Usually, organizations recognize individuals who have character and talent, and eventually elevate them to positions where they can influence the work habits of others. In that respect, the leader becomes somewhat of a behavior model, i.e., s/he demonstrates the type of worker that s/he wants subordinates to emulate. Given that, it follows that the leader should take special care to master the elements of leadership integrity.

Good leaders develop good work habits. We are all creatures of habit, and habit is a very strong force in each of our lives. We decide on the way that we are comfortable doing things, and continue to do them in that manner to the extent that, if we are forced to change, we become uncomfortable. For example, put your hands together with your fingers interlocked. Now take them apart. Put them back together. Take them apart. When your hands were clasped together, did you have your left thumb over your right thumb or your right thumb over your left thumb? Change it. How does that feel? Uncomfortable, isn't it? Now clap your hands. Did you clap your right hand with your left hand or your left hand with your right? Change it. Most people wouldn't clap for anyone if they had to change the way in which they do it. If little things like this are so habitual with us, imagine how ingrained more complex things, like work habits, can become. As a leader and a behavior model, you are tasked with the responsibility for developing and maintaining work habits which are characterized by excellence. If you arrive and leave on time, keep your appointments, conduct meetings in an efficient and organized manner, finish projects on time and within budget, and treat both peers and subordinates with respect, those who watch you will feel encouraged, even compelled, to follow your lead.

Good leaders use authority appropriately. As you learned earlier, my dog at home likes to think she is queen of the hill. Just to demonstrate it, she will occasionally chase both of the cats, who always run and hide under the couch. The dog then prances back to her post, sensing full well that she is the alpha animal in the house, and satisfied that she has once again confirmed it. However, all the dog has really demonstrated here is that she has a severe misunderstanding of cats. Anyone who knows cats understands that a cat considers all other animals, including humans, to be inferior. All the chasing does is generate hostility, not respect. People in an organization are much like cats. Unfortunately, too many managers elect to behave like my dog. They use the authority which has been legitimately given to them by the organization to chase their employees under the couch just to show them who is boss. People who do this may be called managers, but they are not leaders. Leaders not only accept authority, they understand how to use it. This is not to say that a line in the sand isn't occasionally required, or that an organization can run appropriately without tough discipline. But asking instead of telling, guiding performance instead of demanding it, expressing gratitude instead of ignoring good work, and teaching instead of simply criticizing are the characteristics of a leader who has learned the appropriate use of authority. Employees know who the boss is. The organization sees to that. But the boss who comes to be respected, well-liked, and emulated is the leader who checks his/her ego at the door and applies authority with an even hand, backed up by sound judgment.

Good leaders have a well-defined sense of morals and ethics. A good deal of ink has been spilled lately about corporate CEOs who have been caught with their hands in the till, causing tremendous profit losses, and ruining companies. Such stories are tragic, to be sure. But the opportunities for the compromising of morals and ethics frequently occur inside any organization. Leadership carries with it the duty to act in a circumspect manner, always weighing the effect of every personal and professional action. My parents used to tell me to "follow the Ten Commandments, and don't do anything you wouldn't do with us standing right there watching." It was a pretty tall order, but in retrospect, a pretty good formula for moral success. Leaders must tell the truth even when the truth is unpopular. They must follow company policy even when it causes difficulty for employees. They must remain loyal to the organization even during times of disagreement. If a leader is to be moral and ethical s/he must:

- Tell the truth even when it is unpopular

- Follow company policy without compromise

- Treat employees consistently, and with respect

- Make decisions without prejudice, animosity, and/or influence by personal feelings and friendships

- Admit mistakes and stand accountable for them

- Exhibit self-control and courage in times of crisis

- Accept no gifts or gratuities due to rank or position

- Avoid using the power of office for private gain

- Maintain fidelity to both the public and private trust

- Keep his/her private life unsullied

Ethical leadership requires character and courage, i.e., conviction, enthusiasm, persistence, and a desire to do the right thing. It must be practiced everyday so that it will be an effective style during times of difficulty and adversity. The strongest oak tree in the forest is the one that stands in the open, where it is compelled to struggle for its existence against the winds and rains and scorching sun. A great oak struggling in the wind sends down a stronger root upon the windward side. In the same way, a moral leader bears his/her burden of leadership. S/he stands tall, faces the challenges of being in charge, and sends down a strong moral and ethical root, which will hold during times of temptation and inveiglement.

Be the lead dog...

- Employees watch what you do. If your work habits are good, most employees will follow your example.

- Be judicious with your use of authority. It would be well to remember the golden rule during these times.

- To be moral and ethical at all times is the leader's greatest charge.

13

Did You Learn Anything?

Chapter one

1. The right attitude is essential to becoming a good leader.   T   F
2. Anyone can be a leader, regardless of skills and/or talent.   T   F
3. If you plan to be good at it, leadership must be an all or nothing proposition.   T   F
4. Assignment to a management position is a pre-requisite to demonstrating leadership skills.   T   F
5. Leadership and popularity must be synonymous.   T   F

Chapter two

1. Ego and self-esteem can, at times, interfere with leader-ship.   T   F
2. It is impossible to be a leader without being popular.   T   F
3. It is easier to start out "tough" and ease up rather than the other way around.   T   F
4. Anything short of a 100% approval rating equates to leadership failure.   T   F
5. It is not always the most popular leader who gets the job done.   T   F

Chapter three

1. Formal training is not really a necessary ingredient in the leadership recipe.   T   F
2. Training is of no value if it is never applied.   T   F

3.   Change is really quite comfortable as long as you remain flexible and   T   F
     open-minded.

4.   Institutional knowledge can be gained simply by hanging around in   T   F
     the organization and watching.

5.   Re-training is a way to keep up with changes in the techniques of   T   F
     leadership.

Chapter four

1.   "Task centered" leadership and "people centered" leadership are   T   F
     pretty much the same thing.

2.   In order for an organization to be successful, it must accomplish   T   F
     something.

3.   Benchmarks allow employees to measure their degree of progress.   T   F

4.   "Task centered" leaders have no trouble bringing projects to an end.   T   F

5.   Evaluation is a critical component to program accomplishment and   T   F
     success.

Chapter five

1.   It really doesn't matter what a leader says to his/her subordinates if   T   F
     his/her actions speak differently.

2.   Contrary to popular belief, most people actually enjoy coming to   T   F
     work.

3.   Praising publicly and criticizing privately are excellent management   T   F
     practices.

4.   Most business communications fail to achieve their intended pur-   T   F
     pose.

5.   The majority of employees want someone to step up and lead them.   T   F

Chapter six

1.   In order for a leader to fail, he/she must actually *do* something.   T   F

2.   History has a way of sanitizing mistakes in the workplace.   T   F

3. Failure is not considered to be part of the leadership learning process.   T   F

4. Strong relationships do not necessarily contribute to leadership strength.   T   F

5. Good leaders embrace failure rather than retreat from it.   T   F

Chapter seven

1. Visioning can be defined as looking at the parts and seeing something greater than their sum.   T   F

2. Traditional values and beliefs may interfere with one's ability to employ organizational vision.   T   F

3. Most organizational employees like for management to change things and even look forward to it.   T   F

4. Good leaders cause things to happen.   T   F

5. There comes a time when leaders should stop and rest upon their past endeavors.   T   F

Chapter eight

1. Every problem that leaders face is like other problems that they have faced in the past.   T   F

2. Algorithmic decisions are repetitive and well-understood.   T   F

3. Breaking down unusual problems into smaller segments can assist in problem analysis.   T   F

4. Seeking counsel to solve problems is a sign of leadership weakness.   T   F

5. Creativity can, at times, assist in the problem solving arena.   T   F

Chapter nine

1. Minor slip-ups can make leaders look foolish.   T   F

2. Self-confidence is a blessing. Overconfidence can be a curse.   T   F

3. Leaders do not necessarily need followers in order to lead.   T   F

4. When subordinates fail to get the job done, it is the leader's responsi- T   F
    bility to jump in and do it.

5. Good leaders never admit ignorance, even if they are unsure.   T   F

Chapter ten

1. Leaders should always assign the "figurehead" role to someone else   T   F
    inside the organization

2. Employees want their leader to be visible, articulate, and charis-   T   F
    matic.

3. Most employees would rather hear important information through the   T   F
    organizational grapevine.

4. For the most part, organizations exist in a vacuum.   T   F

5. Good leaders ignore outside influences who want a say-so in organi-   T   F
    zational activities.

Chapter eleven

1. Daily troubleshooting of mundane problems is a responsibility of   T   F
    leadership.

2. It is difficult to be emotional and intellectual at the same time.   T   F

3. Problems which are ignored usually go away after a time.   T   F

4. Good leaders criticize improper employee behavior without attacking   T   F
    the employee.

5. For the most part, issues are more important than relationships.   T   F

Chapter twelve

1. Good leaders can usually eliminate politics from their organizations.   T   F

2. Leadership authority must be used appropriately and ethically.   T   F

3. All leaders are managers and all managers are leaders.   T   F

4. Accepting gifts and/or gratuities is an acceptable management bene- T   F
    fit.

5. Leaders must maintain fidelity to both the public and private trust.   T   F

Answers

Although some of these questions would make for excellent discussion in a leadership training session, general consensus is that the correct answers are as follows:

Chapter one

1. True

2. False

3. True

4. False

5. False

Chapter two

1. True

2. False

3. True

4. False

5. True

Chapter three

1. False

2. True

3. False

4. True

5. True

Chapter four

1. False

2. True

3. True

4. False

5. True

Chapter five

1. True

2. True

3. True

4. True

5. True

Chapter six

1. True

2. True

3. False

4. False

5. True

Chapter seven

1. True

2. True

3. False

4. True

5. False

Chapter eight

1. False

2. True

3. True

4. False

5. True

Chapter nine

1. True

2. True

3. False

4. False

5. False

Chapter ten

1. False

2. True

3. False

4. False

5. False

Chapter eleven

1. True

2. True

3. False

4. True

5. False

Chapter twelve

1. False

2. True

3. False

4. False

5. True

978-0-595-39037-3
0-595-39037-4

www.ingramcontent.com/pod-product-compliance
Lightning Source LLC
Chambersburg PA
CBHW021016180526
45163CB00005B/1971